TAPADAWHIRLD

TAPADAWHIRLD

Poems by

Peter Waldor

© 2025 Peter Waldor. All rights reserved.
This material may not be reproduced in any form, published,
reprinted, recorded, performed, broadcast,
rewritten or redistributed without
the explicit permission of Peter Waldor.
All such actions are strictly prohibited by law.

Cover design by Shay Culligan
Cover image *Summit of the Sierras*
(Thomas Moran, 1837–1926)
is in the public domain, via Unsplash
Author photo by Gabriel Waldor
Mountains illustration by Annie Spratt on Unsplash

ISBN: 978-1-63980-818-2

Kelsay Books
502 South 1040 East, A-119
American Fork, Utah 84003
Kelsaybooks.com

for Pamela Grove, Patty Sullivan & Ruth Anne Grove

Other Books by Peter Waldor

Door to a Noisy Room
The Wilderness Poetry of Wu Xing
Who Touches Everything
The Unattended Harp
State of the Union
Gate Posts with No Gate
Nice Dumpling
Owl Gulch Elegies
Unmade Friend
Something About the Way
The Way 2
Midwife vs Obstetrician
Hats Off
Seven Quilts (essays)
Snowy Saplings
Understandings and Misunderstandings
At the Next Table
Time Can't Tell It's Being Told
Beginning Polyamory
Fairy Slippers
wellwhadayasay?
Turnstiles
14 Meditation Prompts and a Treatise on Noble Silence
The Third Way
You Alone Know
Immigration Is the Essence of Democracy
Intermediate Polyamory
The Way Fourth
One Can NEVER Predict the Past

Contents

Flying Saucers	13
Broken Combs	14
Javelina Skat	17
The Right Climb	18
Frog or Cricket	19
Semi-Out of Control	20
Trail	21
Late Autumn	22
Show Off	23
Who Goes First	24
Three	25
Lift Off	26
Oshas	27
Marriage	28
The Tiniest of Prints	29
White Men	30
What stranger	31
Finding the One Cradle	32
Greenback	33
Pika Storehouse	34
Poor Dick	36
A sign	38
Hop	39
Love and Hate	41
Akimbo	42
I Know a Climber Who Is Not an Asshole	43
Two Shadows	46
Twisting Funnel	47
Usnea or Old Man's Beard	48

x

Spring and All	53
Every Rock Is Poet's Rock	54
More Frogs	56
Movements	57
Thicc	58
Puffery	59
Clover	61
Puffball	62
Giant Puffball	63
Good Man	64
Spring and All (One)	65
Two Fools	66
Followers	68
Stone Movement	69
Heart Collection	70
Great Winds	71
Spring and All (Two)	72
Spring and All (Three)	73
Solomon Wannabees	75
A Few Quiet Hours	76
Two Wayfarers	77
Climbing	78
Ego Death	79
Final Instructions	81
First or Last?	82

Flying Saucers

The abominable
snowshoe hare leaves
flying-saucer–size craters
in deep winter snows.
No one alive has ever
survived an encounter
with one of the rare
fluffy giants though
a few lucky ones have
seen the craters
in untouched forests
and marveled.

Broken Combs

What we call a *worker*
is drenched and buried
in honey on a fractured
comb we broke off
from the hive and the
beekeeper, with a stick,
pries the bee most of
the way out
without hurting it.
The bee is on her back,
a flake of wax
stuck to her head;
she's still too
soaked in honey
and exhausted
to take flight. If the
bee's comrades
get to her they will
try to clean her enough
to fly again and return
home, but the stickiness
and cooling night might
just be too much for her,
on her back. We put the
broken comb on a
stone slab now drenched
in honey leaking from
the broken cells, broken
to give us a gift of

a glowing jar.
Even rocks can
soak in sweetness
and who knew it could
be so overwhelming,
even for those of us lucky
enough to just have our
fingers covered. Another,
trying to help, gets stung,
and we are told urine is
a good treatment.
Days before this night
of honey I was stung
dozens of times, on my
legs, and had I been
better educated it would
have been easy to treat
myself. I made a bad
joke about the pee
always dripping down
my legs and my teenage son,
who was also helping,
was mortified I talked
about my liquid waste
in such a casual way.
He had his own stick
and was helping other
struggling workers
take flight that

probably would have
been doomed
without his aid.
They'll make it back to
the hive, but we can't
do anything more
for the bee on her
back. We left
her alone in
the hardening honey.

Javelina Skat

We pass around
javelina skat,
palm to palm,
tilting one palm
so it rolls
to the next.
With pointer
finger I touch
the bunny hair
fluffing out of
the cylinder
and mourn
the bunny's
passing instead
of listening
to important
tips on skat ID.
Though I do hear
there is no
sponginess
to the mass
and there
is a twist
at the end
left by the
closing valve
of the anus.
I need to learn
to mourn
and listen
at once.

The Right Climb

Choose climbs
where a fall
doesn't mean
certain death
but merely
a broken leg
and only a minor
probability
of death by
hypothermia,
waiting for rescue,
high up where
the nights are
freezing no matter
the season.

Frog or Cricket

Is that deep moist
rasping ratcheting
sound a frog or a cricket?
My parents are gone,
grandparents gone
and I'm not even
sure of the great
ones' names.
So there is no one
to ask is that
a frog or a cricket?
Wait! I hear my great
grandmother say
it's neither frog
nor cricket but a
mountain porpoise
that only swims
in the sky above the peaks.
I was so surprised
to learn what creature
it was I forgot
to ask my great-
grandmother
her name.

Semi-Out of Control

One person semi-
out of control
may kick a rock
loose and it lands
on a flower and
another person
in the same situation
may kick a rock
loose and it lands
on another rock.
The rock landing
person may be
violent and the
flower landing
person gentle
in other
circumstances.

Trail

Today we find
just one
small section
of trail,
nothing before
and nothing after
but wildness.

Late Autumn

A King's Crown,
despite the lateness
of the season,
falls for the trick
of a warm spell
and starts to blossom.
Now that I've learned
it's a choice edible
I think of breaking off
the blossom and a bunch
of the stem to eat.
Afterall, it'll only have
a few days before
the frosts last all day,
but I'm finally learning
to leave things be,
even if I have an
excuse not to.

Show Off

You are a dignified older man
scrupulous about obeying the law,
but I wasn't surprised at all
when, rambling around tree line,
just below the lake that supplies
our town, you found a utility
box and pried it open,
hoping to shut the valve to
the town's water supply.
But it turned out it wasn't a valve
box at all but a vent so there
was no mischief to be done.
I'm not sure if you would have
followed through if it was the valve.
Still, it's nice to dream of you
squatting and twisting the handle
counter clockwise, like a little boy,
just to make trouble.
I'm sure, had I not been there,
your prank never would have
occurred to you. Imagine all
our friends and enemies gasping
in the middle of their showers,
with no way to rinse their shampoo,
and no one would know
it was you messing with them.

Who Goes First

Usually you walk first and don't
worry how far back I drop,
but now that you are worrying
about me you insist I go first.
I find I am a little annoyed
and happy and I don't say
anything because I don't
know what to say.

Three

Three people file
through thigh-high
autumn grasses.
The first swings
her arms out like
a crossing guard,
palms open forward
brushing the blades.
Then the second
does the same
and the third,
who is reluctant
to imitate others,
joins the first two.
So six palms stroke
the silky grasses
and when they bat
the ripe seed cases
at the stalk tips
a few seeds dislodge
into the wind before
the wind would have
carried them off on
its own, neither here
nor there as the seasons
drop out of time.

Lift Off

Out of sight a bird
lifts off a branch.
I turn too late
so all I see is
the branch bouncing
like a diving board.
One might suppose
the eddies of air
pushed out by the
branch will dissipate
and vanish,
but on the contrary,
they get stronger
as they travel,
so by the time
they reach the edge
of the universe
they pulverize
everything in
their path—
star dust and stars
asteroids
and valentines
and dandelions.

Oshas

After a hard frost
all the oshas are shocked
yellow and felled.
Their last gasp of
perfume rolls on the air
in a great wave.
I struggle past them,
alone, my only
consolation that it's
easier than it would be
if anyone were to
see me struggle.

Marriage

I follow a lone coyote track miles up
a gulch. There was a recent snow
so it's just our two fresh sets of prints,
marrying in the thin powder.
I won't talk about my stumbling gait,
but the coyote is like a metronome,
except once, there was a six-inch
slide mark in the snow, then all
regular again after that. What a relief
to see my wedding partner isn't as
perfect as I always imagined.

The Tiniest of Prints

The tiniest of prints thread
across the snow, already
being obliterated by wind.
They look like a necklace
that's been unclasped
and laid out straight.
I don't know what to do.
Should I go or wait
for the prints to vanish?

White Men

Yellow Mountain covered
with snow. It's not even
yellow in summer.
At least they didn't call it
ochre or name it after
a dead president. A white
man, typically. We never
let them rest in peace,
white men.

What stranger

kicked steps into the steep
deep snow field so
I could climb easily?
He could be a monster
but he's my best friend.
He also guessed the times
between avalanches.
We're both lucky fools.

Finding the One Cradle

You think you have to travel
the world and spend a lifetime
to find the one cradle, the one
true cradle, just for you,
that will finally set you at ease,
but it may be just off the road,
next to a burned-out building,
where you can spin around
like a slowing top right before
it falls, and it doesn't matter
what you don't know
and everything, at last,
is peaceful and beautiful,
at least for a few moments.

Greenback

You spent your whole
life scattering cairns
but today you built
a cairn to point us
back to the one safe
way off Greenback's
summit block, and as
we passed back by it,
you discretely scattered
the three small stones.
Hoping I wouldn't notice?

Pika Storehouse

How dangerous
it is to make decisions
based on a dream,
but how right Joseph
was about his dreams.
Even animals dream.
What does the Pika
dream of, high
above tree line,
in rippling scree?
The pika, just
taller than a shot
glass, ranges
to gather plants
for winter storage
under rocks.
One granite slab
the size of an
industrial boiler
had a whole bouquet
of yellow old man
on the mountain
flowers spilling out
on all sides.
I missed these
storehouses but
an old man
descending with me
pointed them out

so I could notice
and dream
of the storehouses
of ancient Egypt
filled after Joseph's
lucky dream.
My friend talked
a little too much
and told me the
male Pika is bringing
flowers home
for his sweetheart.
I didn't tell him
I was dreaming
of Joseph,
but I pledged
to notice more,
wherever I go.

Poor Dick

Well into his 80s,
Dick walks vigorously
but with stiffness.
We met on a dirt road
and he invited us to walk
down a steep decline
to see a stream boiling
down a hillside. He didn't
know we are still in
our climbing prime,
spending most of our
days in the high country,
so he warned us about
the steepness and apologized
for leading us where he did,
worrying we would fall.
How delightful that we
say "boiling" to describe
these frigid waters so
recently part of the snow pack.
White water, white
hair, white wisps of clouds
in the dusk. And my love
danced ahead on some
rocks up the steep bank.
She held a fresh sprig
of spring in her palm,
I think a horse's tail
or equisetum,

as the Romans say.
No leaves. She touches,
careful not to injure it,
her palm on the stalk,
and says the name
with a question mark.
She nearly always says
names with question marks.
The water walks down
the streambed steps
with confidence though
that water had never
walked down those steps
before. It happens
to be Dick's 19th anniversary
and it's the 19th of June.
I thought if the universe
expanded and collapsed
enough times this exact
moment with these exact
thoughts might happen
again, then I thought ho hum
and tried to see the brilliant
green stalk without thinking
of Latin or English names.

A sign

in the wilderness
was pointed the wrong way
so we twisted the post
in the loose rocks that
held it and wedged in
a few fresh stones
as it seemed inclined to
twist the wrong way again.
We just crossed five
intermittent streams.
Barefoot. Frigid waters.
Last year's silky grasses
mashing into the mud
of the flood plain.
Silky is an easy word,
but we did indeed walk
on bolt after bolt of silk,
speechless in the luxury.

Hop

A crow, a giant,
arcs down, it doesn't
caw though, it belches,
the healthy belch of
a child rebelling against
her parents at the
dinner table, not
covering her mouth
and not saying excuse me.
There is nothing brighter
in the world than the
crow's blackness—look at it
for more than seconds
and risk blindness.
Its banked swooping
turns remind me of
an old conductor
waving his hand over
a large string section.
Finally, it can't drop
anymore so it sticks its
clawed feet out and lands
on a meadow boulder,
except, it immediately
bends its knees and hops
a couple of inches back up
into the air, and lands again,
presumably, on a slightly
better perch. I couldn't

say whether it was higher
or lower or if it was
like me closing a lock
twice or thrice,
just to be sure.
Then another belch,
and a second later, off,
off forth and gone.

Love and Hate

Winter, walking up
the side of the lonely
two-lane highway.
Now and then a car passes,
some slow and swerve out into
the oncoming lane to give
a wide berth, others
stay in the lane, close
to me, at high speeds.
I love the ones who swing
way wide and I hate the ones
who don't deviate, and I cried
for the young man who turned
back and stopped to ask
if I was ok and needed a ride.
He knew how cold it was.
Even the evergreens were gray
and I didn't thank him enough
when I said *thank you, no,*
perhaps because there was
something romantically suggestive
in his manner, no excuse
for my manners to falter.

Akimbo

A windblown snow bank
weighs on a sapling so
it's akimbo 45-degrees,
the great weight of winter
presses on the few
sprigs and thin mast,
until the cocky plant
throws off the snow
and rights itself. It's best
not to say weighed down
or rising up. Everything rises
and falls at once. A stone
kicked off a cliff and dropping
into the gorge is rising,
and a feather of ash,
shooting up out of a blaze,
straight for the clouds,
is falling, so never say rising
or falling; it's meaningless.

I Know a Climber Who Is Not an Asshole

Today I told four people all from different
walks of life that later in the day I would
meet a dear old friend and ask him if instead
of talking about what we usually talk about
and telling the stories we usually tell,
if we could do something different, if we
could ask each other questions about
what matters most to us.
Questions, back and forth, a loving
interrogation, about the world and ethics
and art, love and estrangement, justice
and injustice, personal and transpersonal,
what worries us, what gives us pleasure. Even
allowing lengthy silences, which give the
necessary space between thoughts. Perhaps
he could sense my urgency, because even
before I stated my awkward request, he was
already talking deeply, with worry and insight,
like he never had before and I could only
listen and give no advice. Eventually
I interrupted and made my brewing
request that had already become irrelevant

by then as what I asked for was already
happening naturally. I wonder if I persisted
so I could tell the four others from
different walks of life that I did
indeed bravely follow through. I'm afraid I
spoiled the mood by interrupting with
my little pitch. He didn't say *good idea,* or
bad idea, or ask if I am crazy. He ignored it
and continued to follow its essence. And later,
not in the deep diving section, but in the time
for lighter stories, he told me 42 years ago,
on a treacherous winter climb, when I made
it up to his belay, frozen, terrified, and I demanded
we turn back before it was too late, and he
agreed, as climbing ethics dictated he must,
but not before telling me he was still good
for a least a couple more pitches, that is,
if I reconsidered, but today, he admitted that,
in fact, he too was spent and wanted
to get down as soon as we could and he
only said he was good for further
exploration after he knew I could go no further,

and his duplicitous behavior helps illustrate
that all climbers are assholes, but he
is most definitely not an asshole, but a
kind and brilliant man. And when he
didn't say anything after I made my
formulaic request for our conversation,
I realized he was kind, brilliant, and wise.
He was also not an asshole when he didn't
try to yell some advice after I took off my
red wool mittens and tried to climb the frozen
face with my bare hands instead of stemming
with my boots against the adjacent slab.
There was no way I'd hear him over
the wind anyway and he knew it.

Two Shadows

I spent a long time watching
two birds soar above
a snowy cirque and then I
noticed I was really watching
their shadows on the snow
and the birds themselves
were much higher,
dark and glistening.
Imagine the snow
melting a little more
slowly where those
shadows passed.
Imagine the two
tunnels of shade.

Twisting Funnel

Once I saw a goatherd walking
across a field covered
with leaves on an absolutely
still day and a twisting funnel
of leaves rose up around
the man, as if following him.
The leaves were still everywhere
else on the field. That was no
more a miracle than anything
else happening in the world
at that moment, and even the
goatherd seemed preoccupied
with other things.

Usnea or Old Man's Beard

The wind has sheared off hundreds
of old man's beards, all fallen
onto the fresh snow. Somehow
I missed all the old men walking
out of the wilderness,
without their beards, young
Whitmans, clean-shaven,
and they walk among us
having no idea they are algae,
fungus, and human.

X

Spring and All

Early spring and there's
a foot of clear, snow-melted
water in a pond that's no
bigger than a T-rex footprint,
and in the smooth mud
at the bottom a few
air bubbles rise up to the
surface and join the sky
and then just to prove
I'm not seeing things,
a few more bubbles ascend
and I realize it is the great
geyser of the universe,
and I am caught in
the geyser for a few seconds,
my body flipping upwards
as I scream.

Every Rock Is Poet's Rock

I was disappointed my dear son
and his dear friends wouldn't
join me on my early spring walk
to Poet's Rock. It's not days
but hours since the first green
sprigs of spring have begun to
weave through the brittle yellow
stalks of last year, and the one
miracle I'll allow myself to tell,
is a fallen spruce, that just today
emerged from a snow drift,
had mature wood ear mushrooms
running all over it. Wood ears don't
survive harsh winters and they
don't grow that fast, and there
have been no sightings of aliens
on one of their mushroom-planting
expeditions. I'll bet the children
have answers. And I'm happy and
jealous they stayed in to talk all
day and night about things both
trivial and critical to the survival
of the world. When I was their age
I walked alone into a sick forest,
brooding. I didn't learn how to
talk as they have, so, when, soon,
they strap their satchels over one
shoulder and the opposite hip,
filled with the few essentials,

hair ties, three manifestos, balm
for their bare feet, and a lanolin-
soaked blanket, and they
walk into the world to make
it a better place, they'll know
what to say and how to say it.

More Frogs

Is it thousands or millions of years
that these frogs and their ancestors
have been croaking here and
elsewhere in their migratory past?
A number beyond comprehension.
Every season they further refine
their calibration for when danger
approaches and they stop their
joyful sexual croaking and bury
themselves in the cool silk mud,
and when I with my four or five
seasons passing by the pond try
to walk as close as I can without
them ceasing their ratchet croaks,
I am data going into their minds,
and perhaps I am getting them
not to stop because I am ever
so slightly pushing the danger
edge closer, and as such I am
imperiling their future because
they should be more conservative,
not less, about when to stop
croaking in this ever more
dangerous world, so I flip back
a clod of moss an ungulate
dislodged, as penance, but my
penances are the most pathetic
in the history of penances.

Movements

One pine needle
half-tan half-brown
not turned to black yet
on top of a giant pyre
of fresh snow.
The needle is
either a long way
or short way from
dirt depending on
if the time piece has
Japanese or
Swiss movements.

Thicc

Through thicc pines
between branches the moon
is reduced to a point.

Just some lint in my pocket
which doesn't even have
the beginning of a hole.

If we leave the trees
alone they will never
leave us alone.

For as long as people
had language, in all
languages, they say

to themselves, to
loved ones, even
to kind strangers,

It's okay to cry.
It's okay to cry.
It's okay to cry.

If we leave
the trees alone
they will never leave.

Puffery

Yesterday, in the giant
spruce fir forest,
puffs of olive smoke
rose out of one tree
and then another,
as if they were tapped
by some hidden hand
to hold their lips up
to the air and puff,
and then great rollers
of the same stuff washed
through the conical
needled stands,
olive clouds everywhere.
Could it be the
smokestacks of
the 19th century?
No, it's pollen, of course,
and we're watching
a giant orgy,
the pollen dropping
onto every tree,
male and female
and otherwise.
And today, the day
after all that sex,
gray smoke from
the Hay Camp Mesa
fire, drifted north,

and sits on the
same forest.
Just smoke with no
embers this time.
Yesterday, when we
finally realized
what we saw, I was
almost embarrassed
to watch, as if I walked
in on people
in the middle of
the same act. Only
perverts watch the love-
making of others,
I thought. Now
I realize only perverts
don't watch. I hope
I get another chance
to watch that forest,
even to walk in it,
and lay down in
the puffery.

Clover

In autumn
when one sees
a clover stretch and yawn
into a white purple
hippy flower, one gets
the same giddiness
as when hearing
a record that
everyone thought
would last forever
was just broken.
It could be a sprint,
or a marathon,
or the places of pi.

Puffball

Is it better for the puffball
to crumble and deliquesce
into late-autumn slime
or for a snowshoe hare
to pounce on it with its
left hind leg, so a billion
or more spores puff out
of the old ball, with a few
ten million catching
in the regal gray fur
of the hare leg? My
answer is easy to guess
but I don't know why
the experts won't even
listen to the question.

Giant Puffball

Some mushrooms require the litter
of two hands to carry them out.
When they're that big it's easy
to tell they smell differently
on top and bottom. The top of
the zeppelin, today, smells like
a rolled-up ribbon before it's
cut and threaded through a
ballerina's shoe. The bottom
smells like smoked whitefish
in my father's left hand as he
makes Sunday breakfast.

Good Man

Am I a good man?
I was the one who
found all four patches
of chanterelles and let
my partner pick and
keep them all. So far
so good, but then I
silently wished that
he didn't find any
mushrooms on his own,
that I was the only
one who could do
that for him. So that
makes me no good,
but at least I am a fella
who doesn't notice
a thing but is good
at finding things.

Spring and All
(One)

We both fell into the
first stream we crossed,
wet shoes, socks, and legs,
so we can walk through
every stream for the
rest of the day without
worrying about dancing
across the rocks.

Two Fools

I asked you the name of a flower,
not because I was all that interested
but simply to have you show off
and say the name, but you grimaced
slightly and said you didn't know
and it threw me off a little so I wasn't
sure if I should ask again, further
down the flowery road, about another
flower, but I did, and you could have
simply said the name, but instead
you added, *at least I can tell you
the name of this one,* hinting at how
upset you were about your recent
failure. I wish you would have just
said the name, but that's you, so
brilliant and worried about your
brilliance. The name? The name
that means everything and nothing?
Bougainvillea. And since we're in
civilization and the bloom is past
its peak, the blossoms have caught
in caches and catchments, vestibules,
fence corners, under car tires, all
the coins of this treasure rotting,
like the coins of any treasure.
And then I felt like a fool for asking
for a name everyone knows.
Just as you felt like a fool for not
knowing the name of that other

flower. That flower which might
not even have a name. Two
fools. That's a big enough number
for us to have some serious fun.

Followers

Follow me then I'll follow
you and we may even
walk side by side, today,
in the cold rain. We knew
it would rain. How many
people in life do you
choose to walk in
the rain with? Just us?
Couple others?
No one else for me.
And we don't even mind
and we're not kidding
each other when we
say we couldn't be
happier, cold and soaked,
in our nearly useless
but very cool ponchos,
with no lanolin at all.

Stone Movement

A man I know moves stones
off the trail onto the tundra.
I place stones back on the trail
and give the grasses and flowers
that were underneath the stones
a pep talk. The other man is
one of my few dear friends.
So we laugh when we cancel
each other out.

Heart Collection

How you finally had enough
and told your partner to move
her heartshaped rock collection,
which had grown to every
surface in the house,
and you helped her scatter
the stones outside and she
was furious until she realized
the hearts belonged outside
in the elements, grown over
by plants and lichens, the great,
patient, heart destroyers.

Great Winds

It is the great
winds that are
worrisome,
ever more
harsh and frequent.
The old ones,
the great trees,
don't know how
to stand against
those terrible winds,
and they can't crouch
in a rock cleft
the way god did
when it hid from
Moses walking by.
Imagine every
tree felled.
Even the saplings
that we thought
would rescue us,
or our children,
at least,
flattened.

Spring and All
(Two)

The county crew has fresh dirted
and graveled the lonely mountain
road where snow-ice melts, heaves,
temperature swings and tire grinding
have ribbed and holed the road,
and in a quiet midnight we
scraped off a quarter load
of gravel from here and there
on the edges. We said to ourselves
it wasn't hurting anyone,
the theft, and we hauled it
to our even lonelier and more
pocked road for its rehabilitation.
No one will know it was us,
and they must look very carefully
to notice someone scraped
some of the new cover, late
at night, and spread it close by.

Spring and All
(Three)

The grand mistress has snapped
off the tablecloth of snow so
in the now gravely shoulder
of the lonely mountain highway
I saw first a glass Coke bottle
dimpled and cylindrically fluted
and I imagined the peaceful buzz
of the woodworker's blade
entering the wood spinning
on the lathe as she shapes
the form based on rough
instructions, the prototype
for the first Coke bottle,
and a foot up the roadside, a gin
bottle, pocket-sized and also
thick-walled glass, with a layer
of wet gravel on the flank.
Of course my friend, were she
there, would pick up the bottles
and shame me into picking up
other trash, but I left them
with a prayer that the Coke
company and gin company
quickly go out of business
and their plants be repurposed
for sober artist housing,
but that their bottles be
collected for 500 years, each
year becoming more valuable

and beautiful because things
become more or less beautiful
over time, and some few of
us have the privilege to
worry about that, which one
it is, more or less beautiful.

Solomon Wannabees

A large displaced bolete cap,
you say, *turn it with gills down
so the spores drop with gravity.*
I say *leave it upside down
so the wind lifts the spores away.*
So we split the cap, half up,
half down, two Solomon
wannabees.

A Few Quiet Hours

The old climbing partners are great talkers,
but the good thing about the big mountains
is they breathe so hard they can't talk.
One stops now and then, doubles over,
and takes ten breaths; the other, twenty.
Forget beauty, wilderness, endurance.
All this work is merely a way to find
a few quiet hours.

Two Wayfarers

One wayfarer finds a pearl-
inlaid pocket knife and much
later, down the road, meets
another wayfarer and shows
off his find. The one who
sees it in the stranger's
palm does not admit it was
the knife he recently lost.
He just keeps mum and
lets the one who found it
enjoy it. Though he feels
a pang for the old knife,
he loves the look of
the other man holding it,
showing off his good luck.

Climbing

The worst thing about climbing
is the climber is trained to stay calm
until the very end, even to the last
handhold before the death fall,
so she can't scream in
desperation, because the scream
itself would be destabilizing,
and there is always a slim chance
the last hopeless hold could actually
work, if they stayed calm, and lead
to another and another and so
death won't arrive until another
day, perhaps far away day.
So don't climb, if you want to
let out one last scream.

Ego Death

There is a concept called
ego death and there are
many ways to achieve it.
Ego, defined as our sense
of self, or perhaps better
to say, our anxiety about
our sense of self.
Ego death simply means
not worrying about
ourselves anymore.
A well-known way to
achieve this state is to
live a long time and attain
wisdom. I have lived a
long time but I seem to
worry more and more
about my sense of self,
as today, with my long-
time climbing partner,
high up, approaching
the Sneffels-Highline saddle,
when a young couple passed
us, despite our good speed.
I was dismayed and then
we caught up to them,
resting, which was some
consolation, as we rarely
rest. But further up the trail
we saw the young couple

behind us again, gaining,
and I told my partner,
with some embarrassment,
that I didn't want them
to catch us before we
turned off the trail and
made for the summit couloir
of Greenback Mountain.
I worried about what
my friend thought of me
for the request, my pettiness,
but he simply said
I completely understand.
Whether he did or not
we picked up the pace
and not only didn't the
young couple catch up
but they saw us veer
off the trail and head
towards the cliff bands.
My ego is growing all
the time as I approach
my end. Perhaps *ego life*
would be a better term for me.
I don't regret it.

Final Instructions

Now that we're old men
and lost in the wilderness,
talk turns to final instructions.
We both agree, ashes on
the wind sound nice.
Does this count as legal
testament, our listening
to each other? Then we
refine the instructions
to say ashes only if nearly
no energy is used to make
the ash; say, perhaps,
toss our cadavers on
someone else's bonfire
that was already raging
so we merely need
to be thrown on.

First or Last?

Is this the first music of winter
or the last of autumn? First or last?
I thought it was frogs or crickets
or some other rasping tinkling creatures.
But it was just a crepe-thin
sheet of ice that had formed a few
feet around the lake's edge,
and a breeze was sending water
rippling into the thin layer of ice,
which broke in increments.
The musical sound was the breaking.
I'm sure ice forming makes its
own sound too, but that's too much
for my ears. I mean, too little.
It was the perfect gentle breeze.
A bigger wind would have wreaked
havoc on the delicate sheet and
the wind's noise itself would have
drowned out any other music,
and the ice would have vanished
altogether in its temporary setback.

About the Author

Peter Waldor is the author of twenty-nine books of poetry, including *Who Touches Everything,* which won the National Jewish Book Award for poetry. He is also the author of a book of essays, *Seven Quilts.* His book *Gate Posts With No Gate* is a poetry-art collaboration with a group of visual artists. He was the 2014–2015 Poet Laureate of San Miguel County, Colorado. His poetry has appeared widely in magazines, including *Ploughshares, American Poetry Review, The Colorado Review, Fungi Magazine,* and *Mothering Magazine.* He lives in Ophir, Colorado.

www.ingramcontent.com/pod-product-compliance
Lightning Source LLC
Chambersburg PA
CBHW031202160426
43193CB00008B/479